DISCOVER!

Animals That SLITHER AND SLIDE

WIGGLY WORMS

BY THERESA EMMINIZER

Enslow PUBLISHING

Please visit our website, www.enslow.com. For a free color catalog of all our high-quality books, call toll free 1-800-398-2504 or fax 1-877-980-4454.

Library of Congress Cataloging-in-Publication Data

Names: Emminizer, Theresa, author.
Title: Wiggly worms / Theresa Emminizer.
Description: Buffalo : Enslow Publishing, [2024] | Series: Animals that slither and slide | Includes index.
Identifiers: LCCN 2023036396 (print) | LCCN 2023036397 (ebook) | ISBN 9781978537446 (library binding) | ISBN 9781978537439 (paperback) | ISBN 9781978537453 (ebook)
Subjects: LCSH: Worms–Juvenile literature.
Classification: LCC QL386.6 .E46 2024 (print) | LCC QL386.6 (ebook) | DDC 592/.3–dc23/eng/20220106
LC record available at https://lccn.loc.gov/2023036396
LC ebook record available at https://lccn.loc.gov/2023036397

Published in 2024 by
Enslow Publishing
2544 Clinton Street
Buffalo, NY 14224

Copyright © 2024 Enslow Publishing

Designer: Leslie Taylor
Editor: Theresa Emminizer

Photo credits: Cover (worm) Maryna Pleshkun/Shutterstock.com, (slime background) AMarc/Shutterstock.com, (brush stroke) Sonic_S/Shutterstock.com, (slime frame) klyaksun/Shutterstock.com; Series Art (slime blob) Lemberg Vector studio/Shutterstock.com; p. 5 Alexandr Grant/Shutterstock.com; p. 7 Petr Bonek/Shutterstock.com; p. 9 Nataly Studio/Shutterstock.com; p. 11 studio kacha/Shutterstock.com; p. 13 Pong Wira/Shutterstock.com; p. 15 Andrei Metelev/Shutterstock.com; p. 17 Image Source Trading Ltd/Shutterstock.com; p. 19 Jonny Wolfe/Shutterstock.com; p. 21 Anna Hoychuk/Shutterstock.com.

All rights reserved. No part of this book may be reproduced in any form without permission in writing from the publisher, except by a reviewer.

Some of the images in this book illustrate individuals who are models. The depictions do not imply actual situations or events.

Printed in the United States of America

CPSIA compliance information: Batch #CW24ENS: For further information contact Enslow Publishing, at 1-800-398-2504.

CONTENTS

Look, a Worm! 4
The Lowly Worm 6
A Worm's Body 8
Worm Superpowers 10
A Worm's Life...................................12
Little Animals, Big Helpers!...............14
How Do Worms Wiggle?.................16
The Important Earthworm 18
Make a Worm Bin 20
Words to Know 22
For More Information 23
Index.. 24

Boldface words appear in
Words to Know.

LOOK, A WORM!

You're playing outside on a rainy day. You're splashing in a puddle. Suddenly you see something pink and shiny. It's a wiggly worm! You pick it up, feeling its small, slimy body. Let's take a closer look at this interesting animal!

You can often see lots of worms on rainy days.

THE LOWLY WORM

Earthworms live in the soil, or dirt. They can be found everywhere on Earth except Antarctica. There are more than 1,800 species, or kinds, of earthworms. The giant Gippsland earthworm is the biggest. It can be 9.8 feet (3 m) long!

In this book, we'll talk about earthworms. But there are also worms that live in the ocean!

7

A WORM'S BODY

An earthworm's body looks like a long **tube**. This tube can be broken up into ring-like segments, or parts, called annuli. The worm's **organs** are inside. Some organs are duplicated, or copied, in each segment. For example, an earthworm has five hearts!

Earthworms are invertebrates. That means they don't have a backbone.

9

WORM SUPERPOWERS

Earthworms don't have lungs. They breathe through their skin! They also don't have eyes or ears, so they can't see or hear. Instead, they feel sunlight and **vibrations** in the earth around them. Earthworms can regenerate, or regrow, parts of their body.

A WORM'S LIFE

Worms are hermaphroditic. That means they have both male and female parts. However, they do need partners to make babies. Worms lay eggs. The eggs are covered in a cocoon. After a few weeks, baby worms come out of the cocoon.

Each cocoon holds a few baby worms inside.

13

LITTLE ANIMALS, BIG HELPERS!

Worms spend most of their time underground, **burrowing** in the soil. Worms eat dead leaves, grass, and **decaying** things. As they eat, worms pass soil through their body and then make poop. The poop has important matter in it that helps plants grow!

A worm passes its own weight in food and soil through their body every day!

15

HOW DO WORMS WIGGLE?

A worm's body looks smooth, but it's really covered in tiny hairs! These hairs are called setae. Setae help a worm move through soil. Worms **stretch** their body and grab the soil with their setae to move themselves forward.

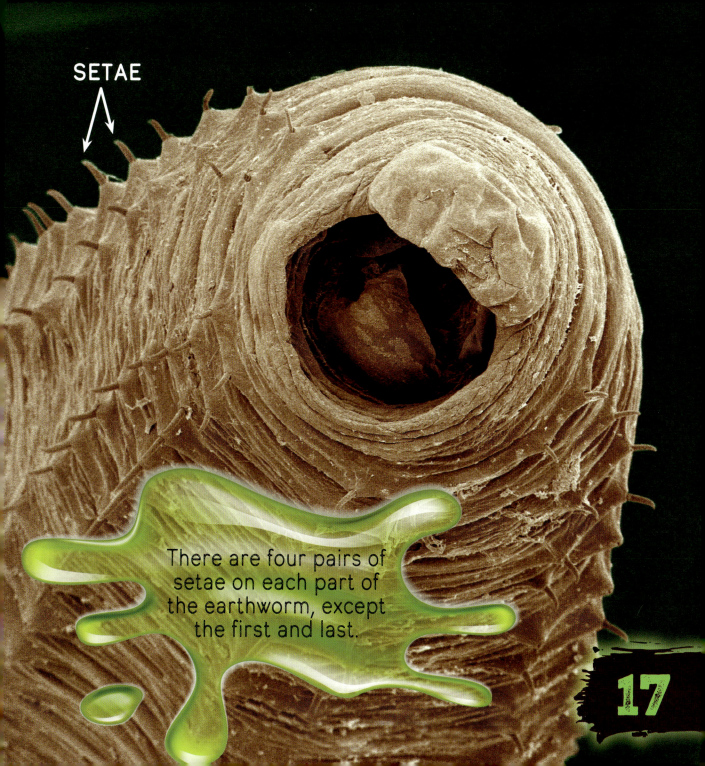

SETAE

There are four pairs of setae on each part of the earthworm, except the first and last.

17

THE IMPORTANT EARTHWORM

By keeping soil healthy, earthworms keep whole **ecosystems** healthy. They're also important food for other animals, such as birds, frogs, and hedgehogs. People use earthworms as **bait** to catch fish. Worms also help grow the crops that people eat.

Worms have lived on Earth for hundreds of millions of years!

19

MAKE A WORM BIN

Want to watch worms in action? Ask your parent, caregiver, or teacher if you can start a worm bin! A worm bin is a box filled with worms, soil, and kitchen **scraps**. The worms eat the scraps and make healthy soil!

You can use the **compost** from your worm bin to plant a garden!

WORDS TO KNOW

bait: Something used to attract or catch something else.

burrow: To dig down into the soil.

compost: Matter made from rotten food and cut grass. It's added to soil to make it better.

decay: To decompose or break down.

ecosystem: A natural community of life that includes living and nonliving features.

organ: A body part inside an animal's body such as the heart and stomach.

scraps: Leftover parts of food.

stretch: To reach across.

tube: An object that is hollow and shaped like a pipe.

vibration: A fast movement back and forth.

FOR MORE INFORMATION

BOOKS

Gregson, Agatha. *I See a Worm.* New York, NY: Gareth Stevens Publishing, 2019.

Lynch, Seth. *Let's Look for Worms!* New York, NY: Gareth Stevens Publishing, 2024.

WEBSITES

National Geographic Kids
kids.nationalgeographic.com/animals/invertebrates/facts/earthworm
Learn more about the amazing earthworm!

Science Sparks
www.science-sparks.com/worms/
Read more fun facts about earthworms.

Publisher's note to educators and parents: Our editors have carefully reviewed these websites to ensure that they are suitable for students. Many websites change frequently, however, and we cannot guarantee that a site's future contents will continue to meet our high standards of quality and educational value. Be advised that students should be closely supervised whenever they access the internet.

INDEX

annuli, 8
babies, 12, 13
body, 4, 8, 9, 10
cocoon, 12, 13
eggs, 12
food, 14, 15

Gippsland earthworm, 6
invertebrate, 9
rain, 4, 5
regeneration, 10
setae, 16, 17